CW00400495

The Mediterranean Vegetables Cookbook

Healthy and Tasty Vegetables Recipes to Boost Your Mediterranean Diet and Manage Your Weight

Carl Ewing

Table of Contents

Coconut Potato Mash 5
Coconut Peas 10
Mushrooms Saute 12
Ginger Broccoli and Sprouts 15
Maple Cauliflower 16
Turmeric Asparagus 18
Chili and Dill Cucumber Mix 20
Lime Tomato Salad 22
Sage and Garlic Quinoa 24
Chickpeas and Capers Salad 26
Quinoa and Green Beans 28
Cucumber Salad 30
Balsamic Barley 32
Mango and Spring Onions Mix 34
Cabbage and Dates Salad 36
Orange Cucumber Salad 38
Lemon Avocado 40
Almond Broccoli Mix 42
Arugula and Tomato Salad 44
Mint Tomatoes 46
Radish and Spring Onions Salad 48
Garlic Green Beans and Okra 50
Lemon and Chives Tomato Mix 52
Corn and Spinach Mix 54
Quinoa and Cucumber Mix 56
Mint and Lemon Asparagus 58

Chard and Spring Onions Mix 60
Cabbage and Walnuts Mix 62
Balsamic Carrots and Scallions Salad 64
Sweet Potatoes and Walnuts Mix 66
Coconut Okra 68
Coconut Green Beans 70
Radish Salad 72
Paprika Beets and Chives 74
Roasted Rosemary Sprouts 76
Creamy Corn 78
Balsamic Squash Mix 80
Cinnamon and Ginger Carrots Mix 82
Rice and Tomato Salad 84
Curry and Lime Green Beans 86
Chili Avocado and Onion Salad 88
Hot Green Beans 90
Coriander Broccoli 92
Garlic Bok Choy Mix 94
Kale and Bok Choy Saute 96
Endives Salad 98
Zucchini Saute 100
Cumin Corn Mix 102
Spinach, Cucumber and Pine Nuts Salad 104
Rosemary and Turmeric Endives 106
Parmesan Endives...108

Coconut Potato Mash

Prep time: 10 minutes I **Cooking time:** 25 minutes I **Servings:** 4

Ingredients:

- 1 cup veggie stock
- 1 pound sweet potatoes, peeled and cubed
- 1 cup coconut cream
- 2 teaspoons olive oil
- A pinch of salt and black pepper
- ½ teaspoon turmeric powder
- 1 tablespoon chives, chopped

Directions:

1. In a pot, combine the stock with the sweet potatoes and the other ingredients except the cream, the oil and the chives, stir, bring to a simmer and cook over medium heat fro 25 minutes.
2. Add the rest of the ingredients, mash the mix well, stir it, divide between plates and serve.

Nutrition facts per serving: calories 200, fat 4, fiber 4, carbs 7, protein 10

Coconut Peas

Prep time: 10 minutes I **Cooking time:** 20 minutes I **Servings:** 4

Ingredients:

- 1 cup coconut cream
- 1 yellow onion, chopped
- 1 tablespoon olive oil
- 2 cups green peas
- A pinch of salt and black pepper
- A pinch of salt and black pepper

Directions:

1. Heat up a pan with the oil over medium heat, add the onion and sauté for 5 minutes.
2. Add the peas and the other ingredients, toss, cook over medium heat for 15 minutes, divide between plates and serve.

Nutrition facts per serving: calories 191, fat 5, fiber 4, carbs 11, protein 9

Mushrooms Saute

Prep time: 10 minutes I **Cooking time:** 25 minutes I **Servings:** 4

Ingredients:

- 1 pound mushrooms, sliced
- 1 yellow onion, chopped
- 1 teaspoon cumin, ground
- 1 teaspoon sweet paprika
- 1 cup black beans, cooked
- 2 tablespoons olive oil
- ½ cup chicken stock
- A pinch of salt and black pepper
- 2 tablespoons cilantro, chopped

Directions:

1. Heat up a pan with the oil over medium heat, add the onion and sauté for 5 minutes.
2. Add the mushrooms and sauté for 5 minutes more.
3. Add the rest of the ingredients, toss, cook over medium heat for 15 minutes more.
4. Divide everything between plates and serve as a side dish.

Nutrition facts per serving: calories 189, fat 3, fiber 4, carbs 9, protein 8

Ginger Broccoli and Sprouts

Prep time: 10 minutes I **Cooking time:** 25 minutes I **Servings:** 4

Ingredients:

- 1 pound broccoli florets
- ½ pound Brussels sprouts, trimmed and halved
- 2 tablespoons olive oil
- 1 tablespoon ginger, grated
- 1 tablespoon balsamic vinegar
- A pinch of salt and black pepper

Directions:

1. In a roasting pan, combine the broccoli with the sprouts and the other ingredients, toss gently and bake at 380 degrees F for 25 minutes.
2. Divide the mix between plates and serve.

Nutrition facts per serving: calories 129, fat 7.6, fiber 5.3, carbs 13.7, protein 5.2

Maple Cauliflower

Prep time: 10 minutes I **Cooking time:** 25 minutes I **Servings:** 4

Ingredients:

- 1 tablespoon olive oil
- 1 pound cauliflower florets
- 1 tablespoon maple syrup
- 1 tablespoon rosemary, chopped
- A pinch of salt and black pepper
- 1 teaspoon chili powder

Directions:

1. Spread the cauliflower on a baking sheet lined with parchment paper, add the oil and the other ingredients, toss and cook in the oven at 375 degrees F for 25 minutes.
2. Divide the mix between plates and serve.

Nutrition facts per serving: calories 76, fat 3.9, fiber 3.4, carbs 10.3, protein 2.4

Turmeric Asparagus

Prep time: 10 minutes I **Cooking time:** 20 minutes I**Servings:** 4

Ingredients:

- 1 pound asparagus, trimmed and halved
- ½ pound cherry tomatoes, halved
- 2 tablespoons olive oil
- 1 teaspoon turmeric powder
- 2 tablespoons shallot, chopped
- A pinch of salt and black pepper
- 1 tablespoon chives, chopped

Directions:

1. Spread the asparagus on a baking sheet lined with parchment paper, add the tomatoes and the other ingredients, toss, cook in the oven at 375 degrees F for 20 minutes.
2. Divide everything between plates and serve as a side dish.

Nutrition facts per serving: calories 132, fat 1, fiber 2, carbs 4, protein 4

Chili and Dill Cucumber Mix

Prep time: 10 minutes I **Cooking time:** 0 minutes I **Servings:** 4

Ingredients:

- 1 pound cucumbers, sliced
- 1 tablespoon olive oil
- 1 teaspoon chili powder
- 1 green chili, chopped
- 1 garlic clove, minced
- 1 tablespoon dill, chopped
- 2 tablespoons lime juice
- 1 tablespoon balsamic vinegar

Directions:

1. In a bowl, combine the cucumbers with the garlic, the oil and the other ingredients, toss and serve as a side salad.

Nutrition facts per serving: calories 132, fat 3, fiber 1, carbs 7, protein 4

Lime Tomato Salad

Prep time: 10 minutes I **Cooking time:** 0 minutes I **Servings:** 4

Ingredients:

- 1 pound cherry tomatoes, halved
- 3 scallions, chopped
- 1 tablespoon olive oil
- A pinch of salt and black pepper
- 1 tablespoon lime juice
- ¼ cup parsley, chopped

Directions:

1. In a bowl, combine the tomatoes with the scallions and the other ingredients, toss and serve as a side salad.

Nutrition facts per serving: calories 180, fat 2, fiber 2, carbs 8, protein 6

Sage and Garlic Quinoa

Prep time: 10 minutes I **Cooking time:** 30 minutes I **Servings:** 4

Ingredients:

- 1 tablespoon olive oil
- 1 yellow onion, chopped
- 1 cup quinoa
- 2 cups chicken stock
- 1 tablespoon sage, chopped
- 2 garlic cloves, minced
- A pinch of salt and black pepper
- 1 tablespoon chives, chopped

Directions:

1. Heat up a pan with the oil over medium-high heat, add the onion and the garlic and sauté for 5 minutes.
2. Add the quinoa and the other ingredients, toss, cook over medium heat for 25 minutes more, divide between plates and serve.

Nutrition facts per serving: calories 182, fat 1, fiber 1, carbs 11, protein 8

Chickpeas and Capers Salad

Prep time: 5 minutes I **Cooking time:** 0 minutes I **Servings:** 4

Ingredients:

- 2 cups chickpeas, cooked
- 1 tablespoon capers, chopped
- 2 tablespoons lime juice
- 2 tablespoons olive oil
- 4 spring onions, chopped
- 1 teaspoon chili powder
- 1 teaspoon cumin, ground
- 1 tablespoon parsley, chopped
- A pinch of salt and black pepper

Directions:

1. In a bowl, combine the chickpeas with the capers and the other ingredients, toss and serve as a side salad.

Nutrition facts per serving: calories 212, fat 4, fiber 4, carbs 12, protein 6

Quinoa and Green Beans

Prep time: 10 minutes I **Cooking time:** 30 minutes I **Servings:** 4

Ingredients:

- 1 tablespoon olive oil
- 1 yellow onion, chopped
- 1 cup quinoa
- ½ cup green beans, halved
- 2 cups chicken stock
- 2 garlic cloves, minced
- Salt and black pepper to the taste
- 1 tablespoon cilantro, chopped

Directions:

1. Heat up a pan with the olive oil over medium heat, add the onion and the garlic and sauté for 5 minutes.
2. Add the quinoa and the other ingredients, toss, bring to a simmer and cook over medium heat for 25 minutes.
3. Divide everything between plates and serve.

Nutrition facts per serving: calories 212, fat 1, fiber 2, carbs 2, protein 1

Cucumber Salad

Prep time: 5 minutes I **Cooking time:** 0 minutes I **Servings:** 4

Ingredients:

- 2 tablespoons olive oil
- 2 cucumbers, sliced
- 4 spring onions, chopped
- ½ cup cilantro, chopped
- ½ cup lemon juice
- Salt and black pepper to the taste

Directions:

1. In a salad bowl, combine the cucumbers with the spring onions and the other ingredients, toss and serve.

Nutrition facts per serving: calories 163, fat 1, fiber 2, carbs 7, protein 9

Balsamic Barley

Prep time: 5 minutes I **Cooking time:** 0 minutes I **Servings:** 4

Ingredients:

- 2 cups barley, cooked
- 1 cup baby kale
- 2 tablespoons almonds, chopped
- 2 tablespoons balsamic vinegar
- 1 tablespoon olive oil
- 1 tablespoon cilantro, chopped

Directions:

1. In a bowl, mix the barley with the kale, the almonds and the other ingredients, toss and serve as a side dish.

Nutrition facts per serving: calories 175, fat 3, fiber 3, carbs 5, protein 6

Mango and Spring Onions Mix

Prep time: 5 minutes I **Cooking time:** 0 minutes I **Servings:** 4

Ingredients:

- 2 mangos, peeled and chopped
- 2 spring onions, chopped
- 1 avocado, peeled, pitted and cubed
- 1 tablespoon olive oil
- 1 tablespoon chives, chopped
- 1 tablespoon oregano, chopped
- 1 tablespoon basil, chopped
- 2 tablespoons lemon juice
- Salt and black pepper to the taste

Directions:

1. In a salad bowl, mix the mangos with the spring onions, the avocado and the other ingredients, toss and serve as a side dish.

Nutrition facts per serving: calories 200, fat 5, fiber 7, carbs 12, protein 3

Cabbage and Dates Salad

Prep time: 10 minutes I **Cooking time:** 0 minutes I **Servings:** 4

Ingredients:

- 2 cups green cabbage, shredded
- 1 carrot, grated
- 4 dates, chopped
- 2 tablespoons walnuts, chopped
- 1 tablespoon lemon juice
- 2 garlic cloves, minced
- 1 tablespoon apple cider vinegar
- 3 tablespoons olive oil
- 1 tablespoon parsley, chopped
- A pinch of salt and black pepper

Directions:

1. In a bowl, combine the cabbage with the carrots, dates and the other ingredients, toss and serve as a side salad.

Nutrition facts per serving: calories 140, fat 3, fiber 4, carbs 5, protein 14

Orange Cucumber Salad

Prep time: 5 minutes I **Cooking time:** 0 minutes I **Servings:** 4

Ingredients:

- 2 cucumbers, sliced
- 1 green apple, cored and cubed
- 3 spring onions, chopped
- 3 tablespoons olive oil
- 4 teaspoons orange juice
- A pinch of salt and black pepper
- 1 tablespoon mint, chopped
- 1 tablespoon lemon juice

Directions:

1. In a bowl, mix the cucumbers with the apple, spring onions and the other ingredients, toss and serve as a side salad.

Nutrition facts per serving: calories 110, fat 0, fiber 3, carbs 6, protein 8

Lemon Avocado

Prep time: 5 minutes I **Cooking time:** 0 minutes I **Servings:** 4

Ingredients:

- 1 tablespoon olive oil
- 2 avocados, peeled, pitted and sliced
- 1 tablespoon parsley, chopped
- 1 tablespoon lemon juice
- 1 tablespoon lemon zest, grated
- A pinch of salt and black pepper

Directions:

1. In a bowl, combine the avocados with the oil, the parsley and the other ingredients, toss and serve as a side dish.

Nutrition facts per serving: calories 100, fat 0.5, fiber 1, carbs 5, protein 5

Almond Broccoli Mix

Prep time: 10 minutes I **Cooking time:** 20 minutes I **Servings:** 4

Ingredients:

- 2 endives, shredded
- 1 cup broccoli florets
- 2 tablespoons olive oil
- 1 tablespoon walnuts, chopped
- 1 tablespoon almonds, chopped
- 2 garlic cloves, minced
- 1 teaspoon rosemary, dried
- 1 teaspoon cumin, ground
- 1 teaspoon chili powder

Directions:

1. In a roasting pan, combine the endives with the broccoli and the other ingredients, toss and bake at 380 degrees F for 20 minutes.
2. Divide the mix between plates and serve.

Nutrition facts per serving: calories 139, fat 9.8, fiber 9.3, carbs 11.9, protein 4.9

Arugula and Tomato Salad

Prep time: 5 minutes I **Cooking time:** 0 minutes I **Servings:** 4

Ingredients:

- 2 cups baby arugula
- Juice of 1 lime
- ½ cup cherry tomatoes, halved
- 1 tablespoon olive oil
- 1 tablespoon balsamic vinegar
- A pinch of salt and black pepper
- 1 tablespoon chives, chopped

Directions:

1. In a salad bowl, mix the arugula with the lime juice, cherry tomatoes and the other ingredients, toss and serve.

Nutrition facts per serving: calories 190, fat 2, fiber 6, carbs 11, protein 7

Mint Tomatoes

Prep time: 10 minutes I **Cooking time:** 0 minutes I **Servings:** 4

Ingredients:

- 1 pound cherry tomatoes, halved
- 4 spring onions, chopped
- 2 tablespoons avocado oil
- 3 tablespoons mint, chopped
- A pinch of salt and black pepper
- 1 red chili pepper, chopped

Directions:

1. In a salad bowl, mix the tomatoes with the spring onions and the other ingredients, toss and serve as a side salad.

Nutrition facts per serving: calories 129, fat 3, fiber 2, carbs 8, protein 6

Radish and Spring Onions Salad

Prep time: 10 minutes I **Cooking time:** 0 minutes I **Servings:** 4

Ingredients:

- 2 cups radishes, sliced
- 2 spring onions, chopped
- A pinch of salt and black pepper
- 2 tablespoons balsamic vinegar
- 1 tablespoon chives, chopped
- 1 teaspoon rosemary, dried
- 2 tablespoons olive oil

Directions:

1. In a salad bowl, mix the radishes with the spring onions, salt, pepper and the other ingredients, toss and serve as a side salad.

Nutrition facts per serving: calories 110, fat 4, fiber 2, carbs 7, protein 7

Garlic Green Beans and Okra

Prep time: 10 minutes I **Cooking time:** 30 minutes I **Servings:** 4

Ingredients:

1 cup okra, sliced

1 pound green beans, trimmed and halved

A pinch of salt and black pepper

3 scallions, chopped

2 garlic cloves, minced

3 tablespoons olive oil

1 tablespoon cilantro, chopped

Directions:

1. Spread the green beans and the okra on a baking sheet lined with parchment paper, add the rest of the ingredients, toss and bake at 360 degrees F for 30 minutes.
2. Divide the mix between plates and serve as a side dish.

Nutrition facts per serving: calories 120, fat 1, fiber 1, carbs 8, protein 7

Lemon and Chives Tomato Mix

Prep time: 10 minutes I **Cooking time:** 0 minutes I **Servings:** 4

Ingredients:

- 1 pound cherry tomatoes, halved
- 3 celery stalks, chopped
- 2 spring onions, chopped
- A pinch of sea salt and black pepper
- Juice of 1 lemon
- 1 tablespoon chives, chopped
- A pinch of cayenne pepper

Directions:

1. In a salad bowl, combine the cherry tomatoes with the celery and the other ingredients, toss and serve as a side dish.

Nutrition facts per serving: calories 80, fat 3, fiber 1, carbs 8, protein 5

Corn and Spinach Mix

Prep time: 10 minutes I **Cooking time:** 0 minutes I **Servings:** 4

Ingredients:

- 1 cup corn
- 1 avocado, peeled, pitted and cubed
- 1 tablespoon mint, chopped
- 1 cup baby spinach
- Juice of 1 lemon
- Zest of 1 lemon, grated
- 1 tablespoon avocado oil
- A pinch of sea salt and black pepper

Directions:

1. In a salad bowl, mix the corn with the avocado, the spinach and the other ingredients, toss and serve as a side dish.

Nutrition facts per serving: calories 90, fat 2, fiber 1, carbs 7, protein 5

Quinoa and Cucumber Mix

Prep time: 10 minutes I **Cooking time:** 0 minutes I **Servings:** 4

Ingredients:

- 1 cup quinoa, cooked
- 1 cup baby spinach
- A pinch of sea salt and black pepper
- 1 cucumber, chopped
- 1 teaspoon chili powder
- 2 tablespoons balsamic vinegar
- 2 tablespoons cilantro, chopped

Directions:

1. In a bowl, mix the quinoa with the spinach and the other ingredients, toss and serve as a side dish.

Nutrition facts per serving: calories 100, fat 0.5, fiber 2, carbs 6, protein 6

Mint and Lemon Asparagus

Prep time: 10 minutes I **Cooking time:** 10 minutes I **Servings:** 4

Ingredients:

- 1 pound asparagus, trimmed
- 2 tablespoons olive oil
- 3 garlic cloves, minced
- Salt and black pepper to the taste
- 1 teaspoon lemon zest, grated
- ¼ cup lemon juice
- ¼ cup mint leaves, chopped

Directions:

1. Heat up a pan with the oil over medium heat, add the garlic and sauté for 2 minutes.
2. Add the asparagus and the other ingredients, toss, cook for 8 minutes more, divide between plates and serve as a side dish.

Nutrition facts per serving: calories 100, fat 1, fiber 6, carbs 8, protein 6

Chard and Spring Onions Mix

Prep time: 10 minutes I **Cooking time:** 15 minutes I **Servings:** 4

Ingredients:

- 2 spring onions, chopped
- 4 cups red chard, shredded
- 2 tablespoons olive oil
- 2 teaspoons ginger, grated
- ½ teaspoon red pepper flakes, crushed
- 2 tablespoons balsamic vinegar
- 1 tablespoon chives, chopped

Directions:

1. Heat up a pan with the oil over medium heat, add the spring onions and the ginger and sauté for 5 minutes.
2. Add the chard and the other ingredients, toss, cook for 10 minutes more, divide between plates and serve as a side dish.

Nutrition facts per serving: calories 160, fat 10, fiber 3, carbs 10, protein 5

Cabbage and Walnuts Mix

Prep time: 10 minutes I **Cooking time:** 0 minutes I **Servings:** 4

Ingredients:

- 1 cup green cabbage, shredded
- 1 cup tomatoes, cubed
- 2 tablespoons walnuts, chopped
- 1 bunch green onions, chopped
- ¼ cup balsamic vinegar
- 2 tablespoons olive oil
- 1 tablespoon chives, chopped
- A pinch of salt and black pepper

Directions:

1. In a salad bowl, mix the cabbage with the tomatoes, the walnuts and the other ingredients, toss and serve as a side dish.

Nutrition facts per serving: calories 140, fat 3, fiber 3, carbs 8, protein 6

Balsamic Carrots and Scallions Salad

Prep time: 10 minutes I **Cooking time:** 0 minutes I **Servings:** 4

Ingredients:

- 3 scallions, chopped
- 1 pound carrots, peeled and sliced
- ½ cup cilantro, chopped
- 3 tablespoons sesame seeds
- 2 tablespoons balsamic vinegar
- 2 tablespoons olive oil
- A pinch of salt and black pepper

Directions:

1. In a salad bowl, mix the carrots with the scallions and the other ingredients, toss well and serve as a side dish.

Nutrition facts per serving: calories 140, fat 4, fiber 3, carbs 5, protein 6

Sweet Potatoes and Walnuts Mix

Prep time: 10 minutes I **Cooking time:** 30 minutes I **Servings:** 4

Ingredients:

- 2 sweet potatoes, peeled and cut into wedges
- 2 tablespoons raisins
- 2 garlic cloves, minced
- 2 tablespoons walnuts, chopped
- Juice of ½ lemon
- 2 tablespoons olive oil
- A pinch of salt and black pepper

Directions:

1. In a roasting pan, combine the sweet potatoes with the raisins and the other ingredients, toss and bake at 370 degrees F for 30 minutes.
2. Divide everything between plates and serve.

Nutrition facts per serving: calories 120, fat 1, fiber 2, carbs 3, protein 5

Coconut Okra

Prep time: 10 minutes I **Cooking time:** 30 minutes I **Servings:** 4

Ingredients:

- 2 cups okra, sliced
- 1 teaspoon turmeric powder
- A pinch of salt and black pepper
- 1 teaspoon thyme, dried
- 2 tablespoons olive oil
- 1 tablespoon coconut aminos
- 1 tablespoon cilantro, chopped

Directions:

1. In a baking dish, combine the okra with the turmeric, salt, pepper and the other ingredients, toss and cook at 360 degrees F for 30 minutes.
2. Divide the mix between plates and serve as a side dish.

Nutrition facts per serving: calories 87, fat 7.2, fiber 1.8, carbs 5, protein 1

Coconut Green Beans

Prep time: 10 minutes I **Cooking time:** 30 minutes I **Servings:** 4

Ingredients:

- 1 pound green beans, trimmed and halved
- 2 tablespoons olive oil
- 2 garlic cloves, minced
- 1 yellow onion, chopped
- ½ cup coconut cream
- 1 teaspoon coriander, ground
- 1 teaspoon cumin, ground
- A pinch of red pepper flakes
- A pinch of salt and black pepper

Directions:

1. Heat up a pan with the oil over medium heat, add the onion and the garlic and sauté for 5 minutes.
2. Add the green beans and the other ingredients, toss, cook over medium heat for 25 minutes more, divide between plates and serve.

Nutrition facts per serving: calories 180, fat 14.5, fiber 5.2, carbs 13.1, protein 3.3

Radish Salad

Prep time: 10 minutes I **Cooking time:** 0 minutes I **Servings:** 4

Ingredients:

- 2 cups green cabbage, shredded
- ½ cup radishes, sliced
- 1 tablespoon olive oil
- 4 scallions, chopped
- A pinch of salt and black pepper
- 1 tablespoon chives, chopped
- 1 teaspoon sesame seeds

Directions:

1. In a bowl, combine the radishes with the cabbage and the other ingredients, toss and serve.

Nutrition facts per serving: calories 121, fat 3, fiber 4, carbs 8.30, protein 3

Paprika Beets and Chives

Prep time: 10 minutes I **Cooking time:** 40 minutes I **Servings:** 4

Ingredients:

- 1 pound red beets, peeled and roughly cubed
- 1 red onion, cut into wedges
- 1 tablespoon smoked paprika
- 1 teaspoon red pepper flakes, crushed
- 3 garlic cloves, minced
- A pinch of salt and black pepper
- 3 tablespoons olive oil
- 2 tablespoon chives, chopped

Directions:

1. In a baking dish, mix the beets with the onion, the paprika and the other ingredients, toss and bake at 380 degrees F for 40 minutes.
2. Divide everything between plates and serve as a side dish.

Nutrition facts per serving: calories 162, fat 4, fiber 7, carbs 11, protein 7

Roasted Rosemary Sprouts

Prep time: 5 minutes I **Cooking time:** 30 minutes I **Servings:** 4

Ingredients:

- 1 pound Brussels sprouts, trimmed and halved
- 2 carrots, grated
- 2 tablespoons avocado oil
- 1 tablespoon rosemary, chopped
- 2 tablespoons walnuts, chopped
- A pinch of salt and black pepper

Directions:

1. In a baking dish, mix the sprouts with the carrots, the oil and the other ingredients, toss and bake at 380 degrees F for 30 minutes.
2. Divide everything between plates and serve as a side dish.

Nutrition facts per serving: calories 191, fat 2, fiber 4, carbs 13, protein 7

Creamy Corn

Prep time: 10 minutes I **Cooking time:** 20 minutes I **Servings:** 4

Ingredients:

- 2 cups corn
- 2 cups cherry tomatoes, halved
- 1 cup coconut milk
- 1 tablespoon mint, chopped
- 1 teaspoon turmeric powder
- 1 teaspoon chili powder
- A pinch of salt and black pepper
- 2 tablespoons green onions, chopped

Directions:

1. In a pan, combine the corn with the cherry tomatoes, the milk and the other ingredients, toss, bring to a simmer and cook over medium heat for 20 minutes.
2. Divide the mix between plates and serve as a side dish.

Nutrition facts per serving: calories 199, fat 2, fiber 3, carbs 8, protein 6

Balsamic Squash Mix

Prep time: 10 minutes I **Cooking time:** 25 minutes I **Servings:** 4

Ingredients:

- 1 butternut squash, peeled and roughly cubed
- 2 spring onions, chopped
- 1 tablespoon avocado oil
- A pinch of salt and black pepper
- 1 tablespoon balsamic vinegar
- 1 tablespoon cilantro, chopped
- ½ cup pecans, toasted and chopped

Directions:

1. In a roasting pan, combine the squash with the spring onions and the other ingredients, toss and bake at 400 degrees F for 25 minutes.
2. Divide the mix between plates and serve.

Nutrition facts per serving: calories 211, fat 3, fiber 4, carbs 9, protein 6

Cinnamon and Ginger Carrots Mix

Prep time: 10 minutes I **Cooking time:** 30 minutes I **Servings:** 4

Ingredients:

- 1 pound baby carrots, peeled
- 1 tablespoon ginger, grated
- 3 tablespoons cinnamon powder
- 1 tablespoon coconut oil, melted
- 1 tablespoon chives, chopped

Directions:

1. Spread the carrots on a baking sheet lined with parchment paper, add the ginger and the other ingredients, toss and bake at 380 degrees F for 30 minutes.
2. Divide everything between plates and serve.

Nutrition facts per serving: calories 198, fat 2, fiber 4, carbs 11, protein 6

Rice and Tomato Salad

Prep time: 10 minutes I **Cooking time:** 0 minutes I **Servings:** 4

Ingredients:

- 2 tablespoons olive oil
- 2 cups brown rice, cooked
- ½ cup cherry tomatoes, halved
- 2 teaspoons cumin, ground
- ¼ cup cilantro, chopped
- A pinch of salt and black pepper
- 2 tablespoons olive oil

Directions:

1. In a bowl, combine the rice with the oil and the other ingredients, toss and serve.

Nutrition facts per serving: calories 122, fat 4, fiber 3, carbs 8, protein 5

Curry and Lime Green Beans

Prep time: 10 minutes I **Cooking time:** 25 minutes I **Servings:** 4

Ingredients:

- 2 tablespoons olive oil
- 1 yellow onion, chopped
- 1 pound green beans, trimmed
- 2 teaspoons garlic, minced
- A pinch of salt and black pepper
- 2 teaspoons curry powder
- ½ cup vegetable stock
- ½ teaspoon brown mustard seeds
- 1 tablespoon lime juice

Directions:

1. Heat up a large pan with the oil over medium-high heat, add the onion and the garlic and sauté for 5 minutes.
2. Add the green beans and the other ingredients, toss, cook over medium heat for 20 minutes, divide between plates and serve.

Nutrition facts per serving: calories 181, fat 3, fiber 6, carbs 12, protein 6

Chili Avocado and Onion Salad

Prep time: 10 minutes I **Cooking time:** 0 minutes I **Servings:** 4

Ingredients:

- 2 red onions, sliced
- 2 avocados, peeled, pitted and roughly sliced
- 1 tablespoon olive oil
- 1 tablespoon balsamic vinegar
- 1 tablespoon dill, chopped
- 1 teaspoon chili powder
- A pinch of salt and black pepper

Directions:

1. In a bowl, combine the avocado with the onions and the other ingredients, toss, and serve.

Nutrition facts per serving: calories 171, fat 2, fiber 7, carbs 13, protein 6

Hot Green Beans

Prep time: 10 minutes I **Cooking time:** 20 minutes I **Servings:** 4

Ingredients:

- 1 pound green beans, trimmed and halved
- 1 cup radishes, sliced
- 2 tablespoons olive oil
- 1 yellow onion, chopped
- A pinch of salt and black pepper
- 4 scallions, chopped
- 1 teaspoon chili flakes
- 1 tablespoon cilantro, chopped

Directions:

1. Heat up a pan with the oil over medium heat, add the onion and the scallions and sauté for 5 minutes.
2. Add the green beans and the other ingredients, toss, cook over medium heat for 15 minutes, divide between plates and serve.

Nutrition facts per serving: calories 60, fat 3, fiber 2, carbs 5, protein 1

Coriander Broccoli

Prep time: 10 minutes I **Cooking time:** 20 minutes I **Servings:** 4

Ingredients:

- 1 pound broccoli florets
- 1 cup green peas
- 1 teaspoon cumin, ground
- A pinch of salt and black pepper
- 1 tablespoon mint leaves, chopped
- 2 tablespoons olive oil
- 1 tablespoon coriander, chopped

Directions:

1. In a roasting pan, combine the broccoli with the peas, the mint and the other ingredients, toss and bake at 390 degrees F for 20 minutes.
2. Divide everything between plates and serve.

Nutrition facts per serving: calories 120, fat 6, fiber 1, carbs 5, protein 6

Garlic Bok Choy Mix

Prep time: 10 minutes I **Cooking time:** 20 minutes I **Servings:** 4

Ingredients:

- 1 pound bok choy, torn
- 1 yellow onion, chopped
- 1 tablespoon olive oil
- A pinch of salt and black pepper
- 1 tablespoon red pepper flakes, crushed
- 3 garlic cloves, minced
- ¼ cup cilantro, chopped

Directions:

1. Heat up a pan with the oil over medium heat, add the onion and the garlic and sauté for 5 minutes.
2. Add the bok choy and the other ingredients, toss, cook over medium heat for 15 minutes more, divide between plates and serve as a side dish.

Nutrition facts per serving: calories 143, fat 3, fiber 4, carbs 3, protein 6

Kale and Bok Choy Saute

Prep time: 5 minutes I **Cooking time:** 20 minutes I **Servings:** 4

Ingredients:

- 2 tablespoons olive oil
- 1 yellow onion, chopped
- 1 cup kale, torn
- 2 cups bok boy, torn
- 2 garlic cloves, minced
- 1 teaspoon turmeric powder
- 3 tablespoons lemon juice
- A pinch of salt and black pepper

Directions:

1. Heat up a pan with the oil over medium heat, add the onion and the garlic and sauté for 5 minutes.
2. Add the kale, bok choy and the other ingredients, toss, cook over medium heat for 15 minutes, divide between plates and serve.

Nutrition facts per serving: calories 180, fat 2, fiber 7, carbs 6, protein 8

Endives Salad

Prep time: 10 minutes I **Cooking time:** 0 minutes I **Servings:** 4

Ingredients:

- 2 endives, trimmed and thinly sliced
- 2 tablespoons olive oil
- 4 scallions, chopped
- 2 ounces watercress, chopped
- 1 tablespoon balsamic vinegar
- A pinch of salt and black pepper
- 1 tablespoon tarragon, chopped
- 1 tablespoon chives, chopped
- 1 tablespoon pine nuts, toasted
- 1 tablespoon walnuts, chopped

Directions:

1. In a bowl, mix the endives with the scallions, the watercress and the other ingredients, toss well and serve as a side salad.

Nutrition facts per serving: calories 140, fat 10.3, fiber 8.8, carbs 10.5, protein 4.8

Zucchini Saute

Prep time: 5 minutes I **Cooking time:** 20 minutes I **Servings:** 4

Ingredients:

- 1 cup kale, torn
- 2 zucchinis, sliced
- 1 yellow onion, chopped
- 2 tablespoons olive oil
- 1 teaspoon chili powder
- 1 teaspoon turmeric powder
- 1 tablespoon mint, chopped
- 1 tablespoon lemon juice
- A pinch of salt and black pepper

Directions:

1. Heat up a pan with the oil over medium heat, add the onion and sauté for 5 minutes.
2. Add the zucchinis, the kale and the other ingredients, toss, cook over medium heat for 15 minutes more, divide between plates and serve.

Nutrition facts per serving: calories 140, fat 1, fiber 2, carbs 11, protein 7

Cumin Corn Mix

Prep time: 10 minutes I **Cooking time:** 15 minutes I **Servings:** 4

Ingredients:

- 1 cup corn
- 2 zucchinis, roughly sliced
- 1 yellow onion, thinly sliced
- 2 tablespoon olive oil
- 2 teaspoons chili paste
- ¼ cup vegetable stock
- 1 tablespoon rosemary, chopped
- ½ teaspoon cumin, ground
- 4 green onions, chopped

Directions:

1. Heat up a pan with the oil over medium-high heat, add the onion and the chili paste, stir and sauté for 5 minutes
2. Add the corn, zucchinis and the other ingredients, toss well, cook over medium heat for 10 minutes more, divide between plates and serve as a side dish.

Nutrition facts per serving: calories 142, fat 7, fiber 4, carbs 5, protein 3

Spinach, Cucumber and Pine Nuts Salad

Prep time: 5 minutes I **Cooking time:** 0 minutes I **Servings:** 4

Ingredients:

- 1 pound baby spinach
- 1 cucumber, sliced
- 1 tomato, cubed
- 1 yellow onion, sliced
- 3 tablespoons olive oil
- ¼ cup pine nuts, toasted
- 2 tablespoons balsamic vinegar
- A pinch of salt and black pepper
- A pinch of red pepper, crushed

Directions:

1. In a bowl, combine the spinach with the cucumber, tomato and the other ingredients, toss and serve as a side salad.

Nutrition facts per serving: calories 120, fat 1, fiber 2, carbs 3, protein 6

Rosemary and Turmeric Endives

Prep time: 10 minutes I **Cooking time:** 20 minutes I **Servings:** 4

Ingredients:

- 2 endives, halved lengthwise
- 2 tablespoons olive oil
- 1 teaspoon rosemary, dried
- ½ teaspoon turmeric powder
- A pinch of black pepper

Directions:

1. In a baking pan, combine the endives with the oil and the other ingredients, toss gently, introduce in the oven and bake at 400 degrees F for 20 minutes.
2. Divide between plates and serve as a side dish.

Nutrition facts per serving: calories 66, fat 7.1, fiber 1, carbs 1.2, protein 0.3

Parmesan Endives

Prep time: 10 minutes I **Cooking time:** 20 minutes I **Servings:** 4

Ingredients:

- 4 endives, halved lengthwise
- 1 tablespoon lemon juice
- 1 tablespoon lemon zest, grated
- 2 tablespoons parmesan, grated
- 2 tablespoons olive oil
- A pinch of black pepper

Directions:

1. In a baking dish, combine the endives with the lemon juice and the other ingredients except the parmesan and toss.
2. Sprinkle the parmesan on top, bake the endives at 400 degrees F for 20 minutes, divide between plates and serve as a side dish.

Nutrition facts per serving: calories 71, fat 7.1, fiber 0.9, carbs 2.3, protein 0.9

Lightning Source UK Ltd.
Milton Keynes UK
UKHW020801110621
385329UK00001B/147